JOURNEYS OF JOSHUA
JOSHUA'S BIG WAIT FOR CAKE

WRITTEN BY
MICHELLE WHITT

ILLUSTRATED BY
JASMINE MILLS

AuthorHouse™
1663 Liberty Drive
Bloomington, IN 47403
www.authorhouse.com
Phone: 833-262-8899

Because of the dynamic nature of the Internet, any web addresses or links contained in this book may have changed since publication and may no longer be valid. The views expressed in this work are solely those of the author and do not necessarily reflect the views of the publisher, and the publisher hereby disclaims any responsibility for them.

Any people depicted in stock imagery provided by Getty Images are models, and such images are being used for illustrative purposes only.
Certain stock imagery © Getty Images.

This book is printed on acid-free paper.

ISBN: 978-1-6655-5246-2 (sc)
ISBN: 978-1-6655-5245-5 (e)

Library of Congress Control Number: 2022903152

Print information available on the last page.

Published by AuthorHouse 03/29/2022

author HOUSE®

Book Dedication

· ·

When you reach milestones in your life that you did not get to on your own, it is important to stop and say "Thank You" to those who helped make it possible.

From the very depths of my heart, I thank God and the community of support around me.

With all my love to my amazing husband, Elliott, and son, Joshua. My wonderful mother Winsome, and younger sister, Melisa; both towers of strength.

To my awesome grandparents, aunts, uncles, and cousins of both the Tugwell & Murray family. To my generous and supportive stepfather, Izzy and mother-in-law, Diane.

With a heart full of gratitude, I recognize the seven phenomenal women in my "Inner Circle" who helped shape my vision. Especially Fabiola, Ayana, and Sassy, who often reminded me of the woman I am.

With special appreciation to my Line Sisters (Spring 2004) of Delta Sigma Theta, Sorority Inc, all of my Sorors, friends (special mention to my Midwood ladies), and loved ones, who continue to believe in me, I say Thank you!

Message to Parents and Educators

• •

As children journey through life, there is so much we desire to teach them to positively shape their character. *Journeys of Joshua* series aims to help to guide each parent, educator, and child through some of life's most important lessons. Journey with Joshua through lessons of patience, helping others, and learning to love oneself through fun and interactive stories. We hope each child enjoys his/her reading time, while they learn these new lessons.

Joshua loved Saturdays. It was his favorite day of the week. He knew it was the day that his mom and dad would do fun things with him all day. It was his day of great adventures.

Joshua was super excited this Saturday morning. Today, they were going to his cousin's birthday party, and he would help his mom make a special chocolate cake! He loved seeing his family and enjoyed eating mommy's yummy chocolate cake.

Joshua was so happy; he dreamed of cake all night and could not wait to get out of bed that morning.

2

Joshua hurried into the kitchen. His dad was sitting at the table reading a newspaper, and his mom was standing near the sink.

"Good Morning Mommy! Good Morning Daddy! Can we make the cake now?" Joshua asked.

Joshua's dad smiled, then laughed, and said, "Good Morning, son, someone sounds excited."

"Good morning, pumpkin," said Joshua's mom. "We have plenty of time before we make the cake; first, you need to wash up."

"Ahhhh, Okay, Mommy," said Joshua.

Joshua went into the bathroom, and his mom helped him wash up. Then, he carefully brushed his teeth, just the way he learned at the dentist's office. Joshua was learning to be a big boy, so he put on his shirt and shorts all by himself, then a pair of his favorite socks.

"Okay, all done!" I am ready to help make the cake," said Joshua. "Not so fast," said Joshua's mom. "Before we make the cake, we need a good breakfast, and I made your favorite pancakes."

Joshua quickly sat at the table. He was happy to eat his pancakes and enjoyed his glass of orange juice, but he still could not stop thinking about the cake. When he was done, he rushed to clean up and put his plate in the sink.

"Now, can we make the cake?" Joshua asked.

"Yes, we can," said Joshua's mom. "I have all the ingredients ready that we will need."

Joshua looked at the table; it was filled with measuring cups, milk, eggs, flour, butter, and yummy chocolate icing.

"Wow," said Joshua. "Are we going to need all of this to make the cake?"

"Yes," said Joshua's mom. Making a cake has a lot of ingredients that we mix together.

Then we put it in the oven and wait for it to bake into the yummy cake that we all enjoy.

"Really? Will that take a long time?" asked Joshua.

"Well, we have to give it time to bake, then we must let it cool down before we can put the icing on, let's say about one hour replied his mom."

"That's a long time," Joshua said with a big sigh. "What are we going to do while we wait? Waiting is so boring," he said with a sad face.

"Do you know why it's important to wait?" asked Joshua's mom.

Joshua thought for a moment, then said, "Not really, Mommy." "Well sometimes waiting is for your safety. If we take the cake out too soon and eat it, it can give you a big tummy ache and make you sick," said Joshua's mom.

"Oh no, mommy, I don't want to be sick," said Joshua holding his tummy.

"If you think about it, waiting doesn't have to be boring," said Joshua's mom as she placed the ingredients in a red bowl. "There are a lot of fun things that happen all around us when we wait."

"Really, like what? "Joshua asked with excitement in his voice.

"Well, you know how you love seeing a rainbow in the sky? A rainbow does not come out until after all the raindrops have stopped. So, we must wait patiently while the rain showers all the flowers, the grass, and the soil. Then after we wait, we get to see the beautiful rainbow in the sky."

Joshua smiled; he remembered how he loved to see the colorful rainbow after the rain.

"What else, Mommy?"
Joshua asked.
"You know those beautiful flowers you and daddy bring home for mommy sometimes"? Asked his mom.

"Yes, daddy always picks the ones with the biggest roses for you," said Joshua.

"Well, first, you have to plant seeds in the ground, then you water them and give it weeks to grow," said Joshua's mom.

"Sometimes, it takes weeks before you can see it starting to grow, but we have to wait, or they will not become the beautiful flowers we all love."

"Wow!" Joshua said as he thought about his mom's big smile when she sees the flowers.

Joshua helped his mom mix the ingredients into the red bowl. He wanted to know more about the fun things we wait for all around us.

"Mommy, what else do we wait for that is fun?" Asked Joshua.

"You remember when we go to the park, and

you see all those beautiful butterflies? Well, it was not always a butterfly."

"Really, mommy?" Joshua answered with a surprised voice. What was it before?"

"A butterfly starts out as an egg and then grows into a green caterpillar. When it's the right time, they go through a change where it hides in a cocoon and then slowly grows into the beautiful butterfly we see later," said Joshua's mom. "It can take many days or weeks for this to happen."

"Wow, that's so cool!" said Joshua. He knew butterflies were special; now, learning how they changed, he could not wait to see them the next time they went to the park. He thought about how much fun he had chasing the butterflies in the park and their beautiful bright colors.

Joshua was so happy. He was so busy learning about all the fun things that happen when you wait, he almost forgot about the cake. "Okay, time to bake this cake," said Joshua's mom as she put the baking pan in the oven.

"Yeah! "said Joshua jumping up and down.

"Mommy, can we do something fun while we wait for the cake?"
Joshua asked.

"Yes, sure we can!" said his mom.

As the chocolate cake baked in the oven, filling the house with sweet smells, Joshua did lots of fun things while waiting. His mom also showed him how to check on the cake. Joshua was so excited to see how the cake was baking in the oven.

Joshua was surprised at how much fun he had while waiting. He helped his mom pack the goodie bags for the party.

Next, he helped his dad wash the car and then his bike. They even had time for a water fight.

Joshua filled his beach bucket with water, and his dad used the hose as they wet each other.

After he got all dried up and changed his clothes, he had just enough time left to read his favorite book.

Beep! Beep! Beep! (rang the timer.) Joshua rushed into the kitchen as he heard the beep. "Mommy, does that mean the cake is ready?" Joshua asked.

"Yes, it's done, but......" said mommy

"I know," said Joshua with a big smile. "We have to wait for the cake to cool down before we can put the icing on." "It's okay, mommy; I know how to have fun while I wait this time."

In class on Monday, Joshua was so excited to share with his friends all the fun things he learned about waiting and the fun weekend he had.

24

Joshua's Journey

Key points:

- ❖ Joshua learned that waiting can be for your safety.
- ❖ Joshua learned the value of being patient on this journey.
- ❖ Joshua also learned about three fun things in his environment like rainbows, butterflies, and flowers that require us to wait before enjoying the beauty they bring to our lives.
- ❖ Joshua also learned how to make a cake!

Next time you have to wait, think of all the fun things you can do to fill your time, just as Joshua did.

Printed in the United States
by Baker & Taylor Publisher Services